Fringing the Garments

Fringing the Garments

poems by

Marjorie Stamm Rosenfeld

Pecan Grove Press San Antonio, Texas

Cover Photograph by Delana Epperson,
used with permission

Library of Congress Cataloging-in-Publication Data

Rosenfeld, Marjorie Stamm, 1930-
  Fringing the garments: poems / by Marjorie Stamm Rosenfeld.
    p. cm.
  ISBN 978-1-931247-97-9
  I. Title.
  PS3568.O816F75 2011
  811'.54--dc23
                                2011043510

Pecan Grove Press
Box AL
1 Camino Santa Maria
San Antonio, TX 78228

Acknowledgements

"Abandon" is available online in *Centaur*.

"A Contemplation of Surgery" is available online at Qarrtsiluni.

"Countryside" appeared in *Rosebud*.

"Keeping a Count" and "To a Daughter Gone West" appeared in the *San Diego Poetry Annual*, 2011-2012.

For Amy
April 27, 1958 – March 26, 2005
and for Amy's son, Jack
January 7, 1996 –

Contents

To a Daughter Gone West

Close, the border near, we stopped.
The West came up between twin peaks
like promises. That spring you carried me.
Your yellow car was heavy with our double weight.
It held the road on land that led us on
till desert gold turned garden, city, and
we saw the breast of night spill milky stars.

You said
I never wrote a poem for you.
Thought it meant
I didn't love you.
Being partner to your enterprise,
I let you go, returned alone.

You phone.
The wires stretch between us, taut like months.
My dreamy head half fills with silver while
cat's cradle calls cross continent resolve.
Yours now the hoard of words I kept:
Brave the New World, finding, as you must,
no land promised but a pilgrim's place.
Harvest the honey of rusty oranges.
Plant wealthy seeds of yourself.

Only then, come.
Mine the mother lode.

Keeping a Count

That was the summer
berries darkened like frowns under the sun.
At night, seeking the wind,
we climbed broad steps,
and you tested a high stone wall
with your light stone weight,
bird confident, careless of falling,
then turned to see the fan of city avenues,
the crystalline of city lights,
the phosphorescent glow of marble monuments,
and a notched sky holding it all together,
so close it seemed you could touch
the warm world with your hand,
carry it home.

Behind you loomed the Capitol,
strong as a fort with old knowledge of standing.
Around its lamps, moths streak and veer in the light.
For you a star flared and fell.
We watched it go down,
drowning in deep trees.

Something I wanted to give you fled then.
From where I stood, holding distance like a charm,
I saw how great when you come to it
the world grows and is out of your hands.

What you keep is a thin volume
containing the declarations flung against dark,
winged things that break the sky open,
the bright pieces let fall
over and over:
our words like white moths,
like streaming stars.

Die Test and Biopsy

The lab results aren't back yet.

White mist hangs over the hills this morning.
Mist in the x-ray of my daughter's chest
yesterday, white clouds obscuring the dark
lump behind. Mist creeps over the road, too,
dirty white, as if the sky is closing.
And I am flying down this highway blind.
The clocks have stopped. The world holds its white breath.
Words useless to amend whatever's sealed
and done, God gone, I do not pray but wait.

Aimée

Summer at the shore face down in water
dead girl's float was what you did, your nanny
statuesque as if she'd turned to stone though
only feet from you. My soul that sprouted
wings, I flew! And still it seemed an hour
till I carried you to where no water was.
Plucked out of waves, you started screaming then,
your living scream the signal you were safe.

Less than fifty years expired, little
more it seems than hours since, in hospital,
I held you while you drowned again, your breath
gone hesitant, your heartbeat almost flat.
What could I do but stroke what little hair
you still had left until your eyes went black
and lusterless?—as if fixed on something
inward, out of reach, only you perceived.

They tell me summer's here, air is sweeter,
say, "Come out and walk in sun." But somewhere
someone screams, and I can't tell who's screaming.
Stone's weight on my winter breasts—can it be,
my daughter, you are gone while I, the fool
who couldn't save you, witless pile of flesh,
live on? I can't emerge in sun, walk out.
I barely breathe. I have no heart for it.

American Social

How old she is, or you are,
when it happens doesn't matter.
At first you don't feel much.
Kindly neighbors, instant chums
come in. You'll need to give them
coffee. Maybe cake. This is
a wake tradition. Never mind
that you aren't Irish.

Later vision will construct for you
how the momentary jangle of the doorbell
shattered the tableau in your living room,
flat pieces jigsawed into new arrangements,
room and you composed differently
each time someone came or went. Today
you don't notice. Make the coffee,
put out Florentines on doilies.
Weren't you supposed to be
sedated, lying down somewhere?

At the end, everybody goes.
You do normal things, bump into
friends and corners. A few tell you
she's in a better place. Wish them there.
In two weeks you will grab your gut,

try to keep its spaghetti strings
from spilling. Some surgeon in the sky
has ripped your child from your rib.
You put on your pleasant face.

Now is when the pain begins.

From the amusement park

each night above the line
where dark has draped its coat
unevenly on trees that huddle close,
the rockets rise. I hear them
before I see them—
tiny crackles
of resistant thunder.

Once, on the 4th,
in a younger world,
friends from India shared our park,
Mina and her dark-eyed brood—
Bablu, Laltu, baby Dinku—
family gathered in with us
on gentle grass. Mina said,
"All of your chilled-ren
are sveet, but Ah-mee is soo,
sooo sveet." That July the fireworks
fanned out so big and bright
they stretched the sky
and showered us
with crimson points of light
and golden coins.

Now where stars
are faint through holes
they've punched in night:
no glimmer of grace.
I am looking for you
everywhere. I grab the phone
and I imagine you. I see your face,
the features change. Flaming globes
of orange and green shoot up,
a trail of blue, a silver sheen
before the previous
has died.
But far off
in an anarchy
of sky.

You are not there,
the child I tried so hard for,
finally had.
You are not there.

Skins

I slip easily into this skin,
warm in the coat you loved,
the one you bought
for such good price—leather
smelling still of you,
something clean
(the soap you used?)
vaguely sweet.

You always smelled
like a ripe peach.
You were that
or a tart-sweet orange.
How many times
in the racing months
I tried to think myself
into
your skin.
If I could slip
easily
into that skin,
become you, let you run
free of the orchard thief
who strikes the globed fruits,

sets up riotous motion,
cacophonies
of terpsichordant sound . . .

Where he roams,
blight, and after—
only the withered fall.

What do I have?
Inheritance: your coat.
And in my mouth,
the taste of a bitter rind.

Snake

And then, from the vacant lot, I heard the dry rattle,
stepped quickly on, close to home and children, safe,
yet even then, sensed the snake's dark menace:
fate, coiled tightly, waiting.

I have tried to undo it each night in dreams.
See how she rises now, beautiful, serene,
the light come back? And when I wake, gone.

Only a strangeness in the grass, weeds whispering
a vacancy.

Venom that stays.

Aftershocks

That fall I went to Poland
was the same fall you were failing.
You were slowly dying. If only
I had known. If you had known.

From the air, Poland is a patchwork quilt—
fields patterned into small, squarish parcels
colored dun and green and gray. You
were done, and green, and gray.

And everywhere gay window boxes
spilled geraniums. I thought geraniums
were an English flower. I thought
that I could save you.

By Polish roads, plaques mark the killings
where geraniums and Germans
covered over crimes. I thought that I
could stitch up sorrow like a quilt.

I saw patchwork fields give up their dead,
their murdered children. The ground
roared, split wide open, heaving children.
And you were flung, a lifeless doll.

Now the shame and guilt of Poland
have merged with grief of you to
a single sorrow. I shake with the shock.
I bear the scar on my soul.

Fringing the Garments

On your birthday, I remember
how sharp your shoulders were
under your white gown.

I grew thin that year too.
Where could I turn
for nourishment? White sheets

held you, white sheets
held the poems
pouring out of me, words

hung on me
like a too-large coat.
They were the cry

which, in the intransigence
of the bitter moment,
I had choked back,

remembering
the thin, choking sound
the newborn makes

when it enters the world,
unlike the last expiring breath
of the child grown,

who, but for a month,
might have celebrated
her next birthday.

After a fire once,
I saw the burned-out stumps
of bushes hollowed by heat—

so little left, only a curve
sustained by a stem. Everywhere
these sad apostrophes of loss.

In your absence,
I am condemned
to sentence after sentence.

With them,
avatars of anguish,
I fringe the garments of grief.

Abandon

Penrose Park

The horses released at last
to flat freedom, we rode
on the meadow of yellow flowers

that went for miles—only the swirl
of a covey of quail kicked up
by whirling hooves, then

nothing impeding the rush
to forever
in furious riding.

I put you there in a picture
when you were 8 or 9. I drew you
propped on your elbows,

chin in one hand,
in a field of yellow flowers,
painted a yellow sun in a yellow sky,

though you had never seen that place
and were riding somewhere else;
your legs too short

for your feet to reach the stirrups,
you bounced, sitting the saddle
in perfect balance.

What may the glaciers carve out next?
What they have carved out now
is sorrow.

I would endure
the horses, picking their slow way
through woods again,

the only occasional glimpse
of a white birch,
the perilous downward trail going,

fixed in the watchful eyes
of bighorn sheep
perched on impossible crags,

to emerge
at the meadow that goes for miles,
the horses suddenly breaking

into furious gallop,
nostrils flaring to meet the wind
on its own terms,

yellow streaming under the hooves
of the horses running forever
over the purloined land.

I give you now what you can't have

I give you now
what you can't have
as my hand curls
still to the shape of your arm,
the warmth of your flesh
remembered, before your flesh
cooled, turned stone.

I give you: Plums
and the branch of the plum
in flower. A star
I name for you.
A mountain stream
the way a stream
runs clear and sparkles.
This poem, my last kiss.

I give you now
what can no longer be lived.

My Son: His Exorcise

It is his tears blending with the water
when his sister's spirit comes to him
as he goes under. She, too, is swimming.
And his eyes swim. He pounds the water
hard, wanting the same water wings—
between grief and anger—those wings
she might have, must have.

A Last Breakfast with Biscuits

I tell my grandson I need a hug. At 12,
he's reluctant I know but complies anyway.
He will fly home this morning. Now that he's left
I feel empty and order two rosemary biscuits—
one I can gulp down here. On the ground near the feet

of outdoor customers, sparrows are jerking around
like toy automatons, flinging themselves at crumbs.
A waitress brings me a bag with my second
rosemary biscuit. For a moment, imagine there are
no seconds. No second servings, no second chances,

no other place. In this case, would you take
more than your share? A table away,
are generous neighbors. They are breaking off
tiny, bite-sized bits of a scone for birds
who plop down on their table. For the birds

it is always Now; Here is wherever they are.
Would you want to be solely spirit, incorporeal,
hovering on clouds? Nothing to sate your hunger,
no sight of familiar faces? No holy communion
of flesh? As if of one mind, the birds rise in a flurry

above us. In the air they seem full of grace.
I am making my mind indifferent. Neutral
as the bloody beating heart of a bird. I try
to obliterate Later. I ravish two rosemary biscuits
as if this is the only feast I am ever going to have.

A Contemplation of Surgery

Old eye. A window and its pane. Whether
what clouds it now is cataracts or grief: the knife.
Clean swipe. The pane, the pain. Then clarity.

Woods: The Way through

Yes. These woods tug at you.
Going past, we go deeper and deeper.
You take this on faith.
After blind access,
a road like a closed loop
leading us God-knows-where,
the Freeway. Or here
in the woods we choose,
imagine you lay your winter hand
on the whorl of a young dogwood,
knowing how heritage *will* come
hard on its heel, how beyond trees
the quiet leaves bear on a broad stream,
credit to when (how soon!) a white
bravery of blossoms springs loose,
the wood lace wakeful, wild,
asserting itself past sleep.

Countryside

After long misery, surcease.

Beside our roads,
leaves change in light to tell our history.
Trees hang heavy with the wet glint of apples.
The banked fields rise, birds low over the levee,
the sun tangled in wheat.

And in this sage and golden land,
all streams run down to the same cynosure:

Peace.
And the knowing we have come home.

Intaglio

The sky, translucent now with apricot light
not yet fading into evening,
the sea, creamy near the shore.
Your footprint, deep where your heel struck sand,
the impression of your toes, a small fan
like the most delicate scalloped shell.

I ask the waves not to wipe away
the sign that we were here.

2011-2012 BOOKS FROM PECAN GROVE PRESS

Challender, Craig. *As Details Become Available.* 2012.
ISBN: 978-1-937302-01-6 $15

Haddad, Marian. *Wildflower. Stone.* 2011.
ISBN: 1-978-931247-88-7 (paper) $15
ISBN: 978-1-931247-85-6 (cloth) $25

Heinzelman, Kurt. *The Names They Found There.* 2011.
ISBN: 978-1-931247-27-0 $15

Hotham,. Gary. *Nothing More Happens in the Twentieth Century.* 2012.
ISBN: 978-1-93124798-6 $7

Kolosoz, Jacqueline. *Hourglass.* 2012.
ISBN: 978-1-937302-02-3 $7

Levin, Carol. *Stunned by the Velocity.* 2012.
ISBN: 978-1-937302-03-0 $15

Lyons, Bonnie. *Bedrock.* 2011.
ISBN: 978-1-931247-83-2 $15

McFarland, Ron. *Subtle Thieves.* 2012.
ISBN: 978-1-931247-99-3 $15

Randall, Jessy & Daniel M. Shapiro. *Interruptions.* 2011.
ISBN: 978-1-931247-90-0 $15

Scudder, Emily, *Feeding Time.* 2011.
ISBN: 978-1-931247-91-7 $15

Siedlarz, Lisa L., *What We Sign Up For.* 2011.
ISBN: 978-1-931247-96-2 $15

Simon, Beth. *No Mirror, No Hunger.* 2012.
ISBN: 978-1-931247-94-8 (paper) $15
ISBN: 978-1-931247-93-1 (cloth) $23

Starkey, David. *It Must Be Like the World.* 2011.
ISBN: 978-1-931247084-9 $15

Valdata, Pat. *Inherent Vice.* 2011.
ISBN: 978-1-931247-30-6 $15

Wiggerman, Scott. *Presence.* 2011.
ISBN: 978-1-931247-95-5 $15

Wing, Avra. *Recurring Dream.* 2011.
ISBN: 978-1-931247-92-4 $7

To see all available Pecan Grove Press Books from 1988-2012),
please visit our website at **http://library.stmarytx.edu/pgpress**